Slap & Pop Bass

A Guide to Modern Funk Techniques

Alfred, the leader in educational publishing, and the National Guitar Workshop, one of America's finest guitar schools, have joined forces to bring you the best, most progressive educational tools possible. We hope you will enjoy this book and encourage you to look for other fine products from Alfred and the National Guitar Workshop.

ISBN 0-7390-2815-4 (Book and CD)

This book was acquired, edited and produced by Workshop Arts, Inc., the publishing arm of the National Guitar Workshop.
Nathaniel Gunod, acquisitions and editor
Michael Rodman, editor
Matthew Cramer, music typesetter
Tim Phelps, interior design and photography
CD recorded at Bar None Studios in Northford, CT

DAVID OVERTHROW

TABLE OF CONTENTS

A compact disc is included with this book. This disc can make learning with the book easier and more enjoyable. The symbol shown at the left appears next to every example that is on the CD. Use the CD to help ensure that you're capturing the feel of the examples and interpreting the rhythms correctly. The numeral below the symbol corresponds directly to the CD track number. Track 1 provides tuning notes for your bass.

ABOUT THE AUTHORS

David Overthrow has been a bass performer and instructor since the 1980s. He studied at Berklee College of Music and later earned a Bachelor of Music degree from Western Connecticut State University. Dave has been a member of the bass faculty at the National Guitar Workshop since 1984. He is presently Director of Music and Head of Jazz Studies at the Canterbury School in New Milford, Connecticut, and performs regularly in New York City and Connecticut. In addition to appearing on several CDs in styles ranging from funk to rock to reggae, Dave records with his own band, HIPpOCKET. He has performed with such artists as Mike Stern, John Abercrombie, Trey Anastasio, Larry Coryell and Zakk Wylde.

David Overthrow endorses R&B basses, DR Handmade Strings and SWR Bass Amplifiers.

PHOTO BY HEIDI JOHNSON

INTRODUCTION

The slap & pop technique has been used by players for decades and has evolved into one of the most exciting styles of electric bass playing. Larry Graham of Grand Funk Railroad was one of the pioneers in the early stages. Over the years, great players such as Stanley Clark, Daryl Jones, Mark King, Marcus Miller and Victor Wooten have taken slap & pop to new levels of virtuosity.

Slap & pop actually involves several techniques. Larry Graham used the slap technique in the 1960s; the pop was later added and became a crucial element, providing for more exciting bass lines. Other techniques that are important to the slap & pop style are muted notes, hammer-ons, pull-offs and slides. Modern players also use double pops and popped double stops. All of these techniques are covered in this book.

This book is designed for students of intermediate to advanced levels and methodically introduces the techniques of slap & pop. For example, Chapter 3 is full of bass lines using just slap technique. The next chapter introduces the pop technique and provides many slap & pop bass lines. Through this process, you will learn the many techniques used in slap & pop and also play through some great, funky bass lines. The book assumes you play the electric bass already and, while there is a brief review of the basics, it is best if you already read standard music notation and/or tablature, and have experience reading complex rhythms including sixteenth notes, triplets, dotted notes and so on.

I have seen many books about slap & pop bass, none of which fully address each technique involved. Since each chapter addresses a particular technique and provides some great bass lines, this book is particularly helpful for intermediate players. Advanced players may have more experience with each of the techniques, but will certainly enjoy learning all of the funk bass grooves provided. Chapters 5 poses more of a challenge for the advanced player, since the hammer-ons and pull-offs allow for some incredibly funky lines. Chapter 6 discusses double pops, popped double stops and double slides. Chapter 7 is a library of funk bass lines drawing from all of the techniques discussed in the book.

No matter what your level, you should go through the book in order, from the beginning. Even many of the bass lines that use just the slap technique are good funk grooves and worth learning. Play through all of the examples very slowly at first, making sure you get a clean sound and that you are playing the rhythms correctly.

This book is just one resource of many to help you become a better bass player. Use it along with other books from the National Guitar Workshop and Alfred, such as *The Complete Electric Bass Method, Building Bass Lines* and *30-Day Bass Workout,* to improve both as a musician and as a bass player. Most important, learn as many tunes as possible and play with other musicians as often as possible. There is no substitute for jamming and performing with other musicians.

ACKNOWLEDGEMENTS
I would like to thank: My wonderful mother; my brother Keith; Yvette; Dave Smolover and Nat Gunod from the National Guitar Workshop; builder Ron Blake and his partner Ed Roman at R&B basses (www.worldclassguitars.com) for building my wonderful basses. Also, thanks to Dave from SWR and Malcom from DR. A special thanks goes to my friend Aaron Scott for finding time between tours with the great jazz pianist McCoy Tyner to play drums on the CD for this book.

CHAPTER 1
A REVIEW OF THE BASICS

This chapter is a review of basic materials and concepts that are covered in *Beginning Electric Bass,* also from the National Guitar Workshop and Alfred. If you already read music and tablature, know how to find every note on the bass and have completed *Beginning Electric Bass,* you can skip this chapter and begin with Chapter 2 on page 10.

READING MUSIC

THE STAFF
Music is written on the *staff,* which consists of five lines and four spaces.

THE BASS CLEF
This sign 𝄢 is the *bass clef.* The dots surround the 4th line of the staff, which is desgnated as the note "F." For that reason, this clef is often called the *F clef.* Most electric bass music is written in the bass clef. The notes on the bass clef staff are as follows:

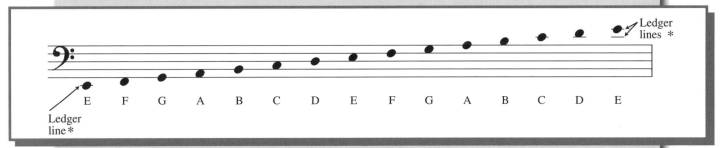

*Ledger lines are used to show notes that are too high or too low for the staff.

MEASURES AND BAR LINES
Bar lines divide the staff into *measures.* Each measure contains an equal number of *beats.* A beat is the basic unit of musical time. The *double bar line* indicates the end of a section or example.

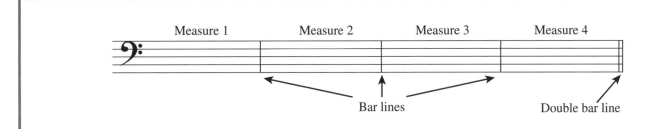

NOTES AND RESTS

Here is a review of note and rest values:

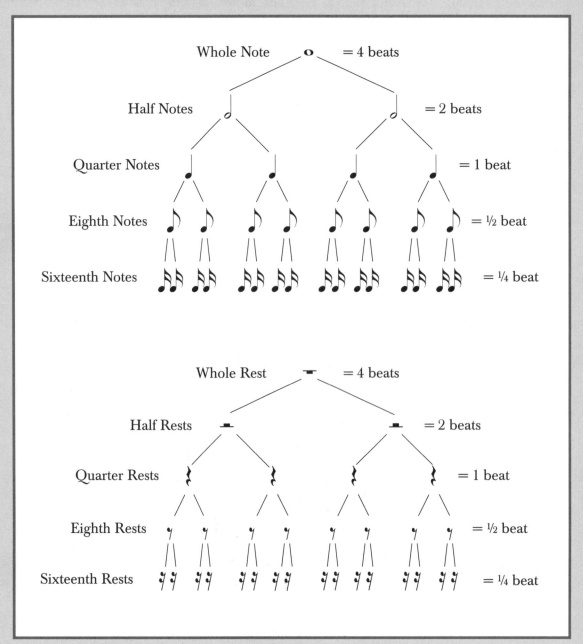

TIME SIGNATURES

The *time signature* consists of two numbers at the beginning of a staff, to the right of the clef. The top number indicates how many beats are in each measure. The bottom number tells you what kind of note gets one beat.

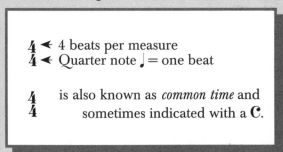

THE TIE

A *tie* is a curved line between two notes of the same pitch. The first note is played and held for the duration of both: The second note is not struck; rather, its value is added to that of the first.

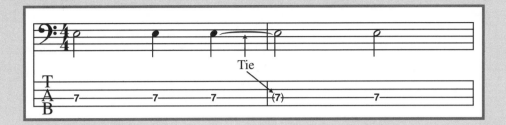

DOTTED NOTES

Adding a dot to the right of a note increases the note's value by one-half. For example, a half note equals two beats. Half of that value is one beat, which is the value of a quarter note. So, a dotted half note is like a half note tied to a quarter note:

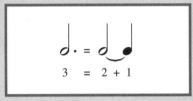

A quarter note equals one beat. Half of that value is one-half beat, which is the value of an eighth note. So, a dotted quarter note is like a quarter note tied to an eighth note:

If you study the chart below, you will see that the dotted quarter note has the same time value as the three eighth notes it is compared to. The dotted half note has the same time value as the three quarter notes it is compared to.

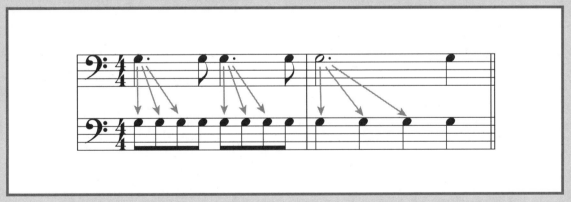

TRIPLETS

A triplet is a group of three notes played in the time of two. For example,

an eighth-note triplet 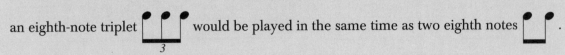 would be played in the same time as two eighth notes .

When counting triplets, think of a three-syllable word or phrase. This will help you divide the beat into three equal parts. The following works well:

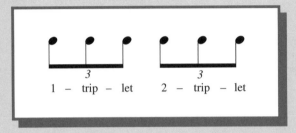

1 – trip – let   2 – trip – let

Here are some other examples of triplets:

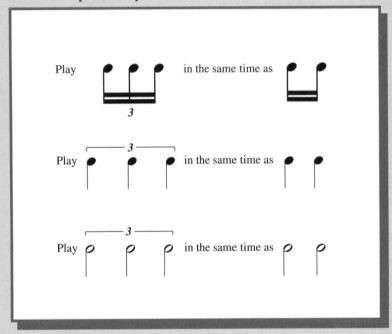

Play   in the same time as

Play   in the same time as

Play   in the same time as

SLAP & POP NOTATION

Several symbols are used to indicate the different types of slap & pop techniques in both standard music notation and TAB. The following key shows the symbols for the various techniques used in this book.

S	=	Slap
P	=	Pop
H	=	Hammer-on
PO	=	Pull-off
SL	=	Slide
×	=	Muted note
P / P	=	Popped Double Stop
SL / SL	=	Double slide

The example below is a typical two-bar slap & pop bass line demonstrating some of the most common techniques and their notation.

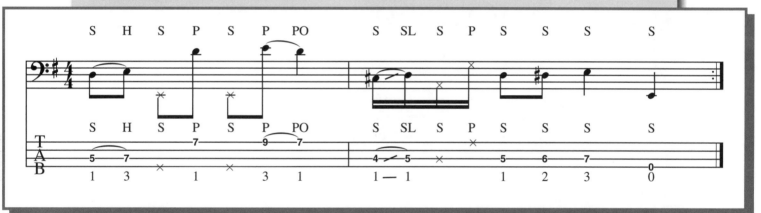

That's all the review and preparation we have space for. If you need more basic information about reading music for and playing the electric bass, read *Beginning Electric Bass*, also published by the National Guitar Workshop and Alfred.

CHAPTER 2
AN OVERVIEW OF THE BASIC TECHNIQUES

Think of each slap & pop technique you learn as being like a different drum in a drum kit. Each drum adds a different color to a great drum groove. Likewise, each technique adds to a new color to a slap & pop bass line. The techniques become the palette from which you create colorful, funky bass lines.

THE SLAP

The *slap* is executed by using the lower side of the thumb to strike the string. Allow the thumb to bounce off of the string to avoid stopping the string. It is important to get a good percussive sound when slapping the string and then sustain the note. It is equally important to stop the note from ringing when you are done with it, thus avoiding the common problem of background noise.

The angle at which you hold the hand when slapping is one of personal preference. Here are two common slapping positions. Use whichever way works best for you.

Slap Position #1

Most players prefer slap position #1. Holding the hand this way makes it easier to follow the slap with a pop.

Slap Position #2

THE POP

The *pop* is the most distinctive sound in a slap & pop bass line. A pop is executed by placing the index finger of the right hand underneath the string (usually the 1st or 2nd string) and pulling it away from the fingerboard, allowing it to snap back against the frets. This produces a very percussive sound, more so than the slap.

Here are pictures showing the two hand positions that can be used when popping strings.

Pop Position #1

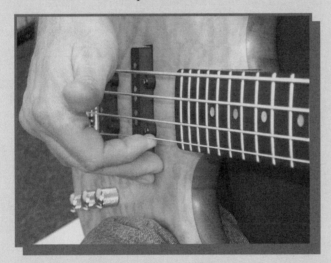

Pop Position #2

__Marcus Miller__ began his career in the late 1970s, working with saxophonist Dave Sanborn. He later worked with singer Luther Vandross, and recorded six albums with jazz icon Miles Davis in the late 1980s.

HAMMER-ONS AND PULL-OFFS

Hammer-ons and *pull-offs* add interest and excitement to your bass lines. These techniques allow for fast, fluid lines. Listen to the work of Victor Wooten (Bela Fleck and the Flecktones, and solo albums) to hear some amazing slap & pop playing with lots of hammer-ons and pull-offs. Hammer-ons and pull-offs are *legato* techniques; they allow for a smooth connection between notes without striking the string with the right hand. They are written with a *slur*, which is curved line, and an "H" for hammer-on or a "P" for pull-off.

HAMMER-ONS

The hammer-on is executed by tapping the string with the left-hand finger to sound a higher-pitched note without plucking with the right hand. For example, play the D on the 5th fret of the 3rd string with the 1st finger of the left hand. Now, tap the string on the 7th fret with the 3rd finger with enough force to cause the E on the 7th fret to sound without using the right hand at all. When you succeed, you have played a hammer-on.

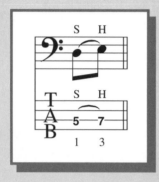

PULL-OFFS

A pull-off is executed by yanking a left-hand finger slightly downward and away from a fin-gered note to cause a lower-pitched note (fretted or open) to sound without plucking with the right hand. For example, play the E on the 7th fret of the 3rd string with the 3rd finger while also holding the D on the 5th fret with the 1st finger. Pull the 3rd finger away from the string (snap it–don't just pick it up) with enough force to cause the D on the 5th fret to sound without using the right hand at all. When you have succeeded, you have played a pull-off.

Pull-offs frequently follow hammer-ons.

MUTED, OR DEAD NOTES

The *muted*, or *dead* note is an integral part of your palette of colors and helps provide for some very funky bass lines. It is played by placing the fingers of your left hand against the string without pressing it to the fingerboard. Playing a muted string creates a percussive, quasi-pitch sound. Make sure that you dampen the strings with two or more fingers; using only one finger can generate a harmonic, which is a very different effect.

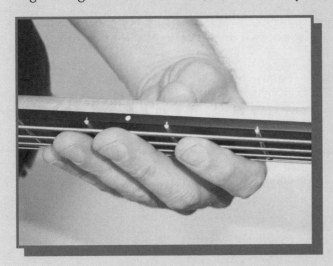

Muting the strings

Muted notes are written as follows:

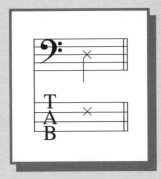

SLIDES

A slide is a very expressive technique, and is another cool way to create a legato sound. Two notes on the same string are connected by simply gliding a left-hand finger up or down from one fret to another. This creates an almost vocal, sliding sound. Usually, the second note in a slide is not articulated with the right hand, so the two notes are connected with a slur. An ascending or descending line and the letters SL are used to indicate the slide.

Here are typical ascending and descending slides.

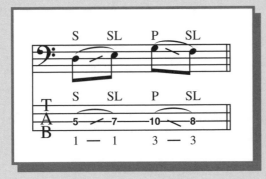

CHAPTER 3
THE SLAP

As discussed on page 10, the slap is executed by using the lower side of the thumb to strike the string. One of the most important aspects of slap & pop bass playing is having control over each note. After playing a note, it is important to stop it from ringing before playing the next. This is especially important when you are playing bass lines that involve several strings.

It may take you a while to get a clear slap tone. If you have never tried the slap technique before, take the time to work on making a good tone when playing these open string exercises before continuing to work through the book. Experiment with your hand position and the force required to make a clear tone.

Below are exercises on open strings. Be sure to strike the string with the lower side of your thumb as cleanly as possible and avoid hitting other strings. Remember to play slowly at first, then practice at faster *tempos* (speeds).

SLAPPING EXERCISES ON OPEN STRINGS

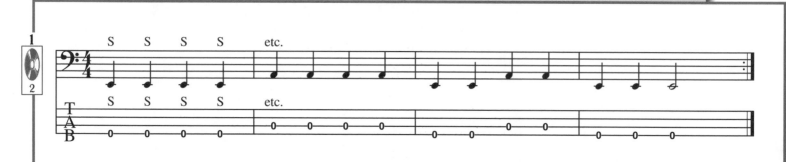

Here are more exercises on open strings. Make sure to stop each note just before slapping the next. Pay close attention to the eighth-note rhythms.

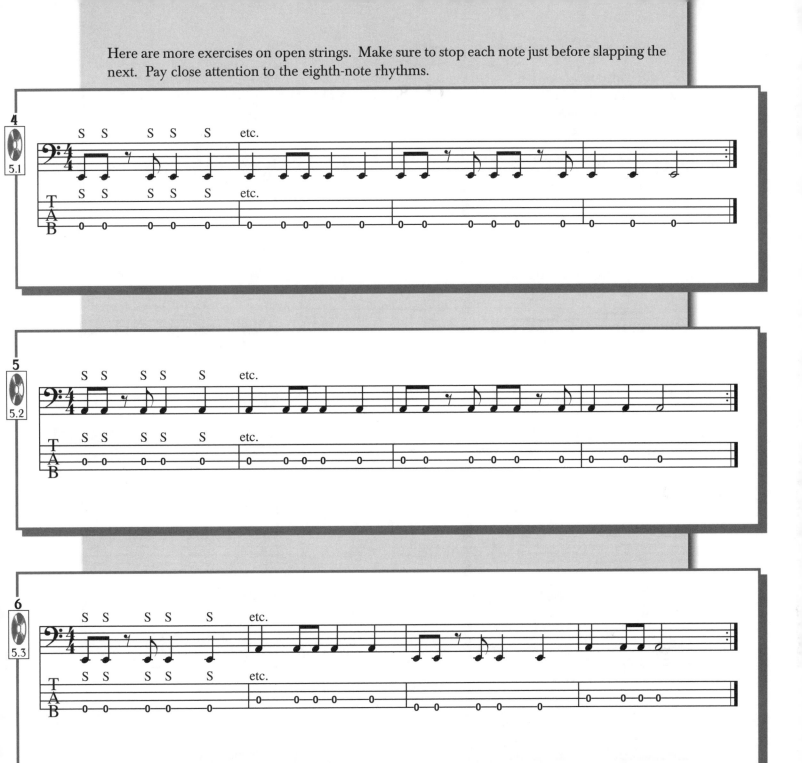

ONE-BAR SLAPPING LICKS

Following are 12 one-bar bass licks using the slap technique. Since every note is slapped, the S is not used in the notation. Make sure to play each example slowly at first. When you feel confident, increase the tempo. Also, notice that some notes are muted (×).

TWO-BAR SLAPPING LICKS

Pay close attention to playing the correct rhythms, executing the muted notes and producing a clear tone.

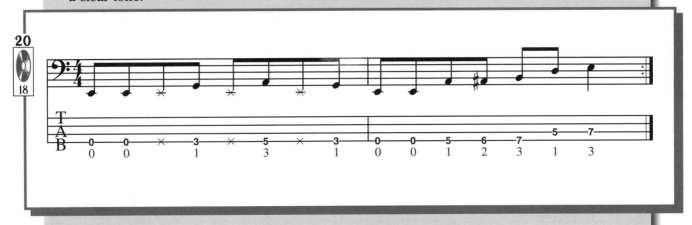

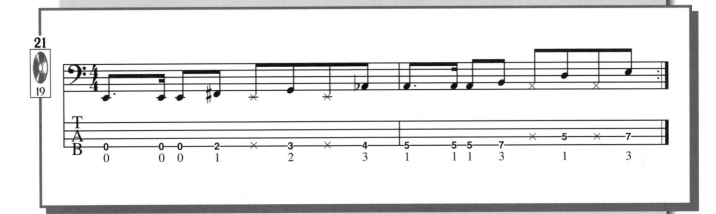

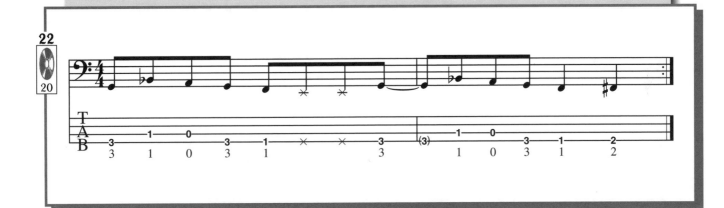

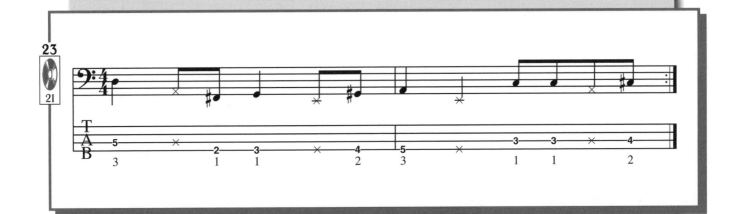

FOUR-BAR SLAPPING GROOVES

Here are two four-bar slap grooves. It is a good idea to play them with a drum machine or metronome. It is also important to lock into the pulse and provide a good groove.

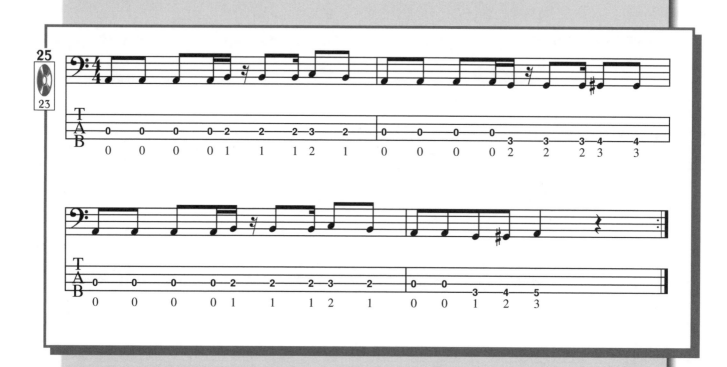

CHAPTER 4
THE POP

The pop is of equal or even greater importance than the slap to the slap & pop style because it so distinctive sounding. The pop produces a much more percussive sound than the slap. As described on page 11, the string is pulled away from the fingerboard, and when released, snaps back with great force against the frets.

Use the 1st finger to pop the string. The popping technique is commonly used on the 1st string (G) and 2nd string (D) of the bass. Refer to page 11 for information about the popping hand position. Experiment with both hand positions shown and see which you prefer.

POPPING EXERCISES ON OPEN STRINGS

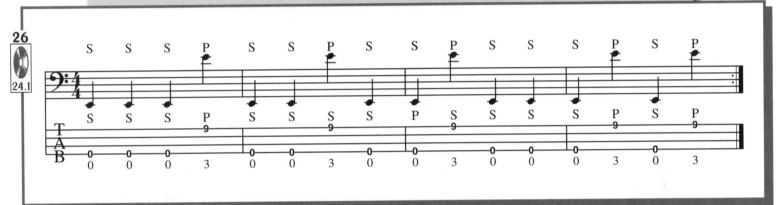

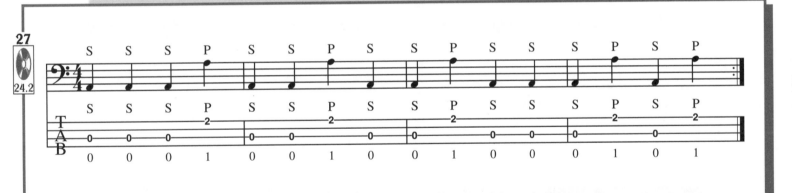

ONE-BAR SLAP & POP LICKS

Now that you are mixing slaps and pops, it is even more important to practice slowly at first and build up to quicker tempos.

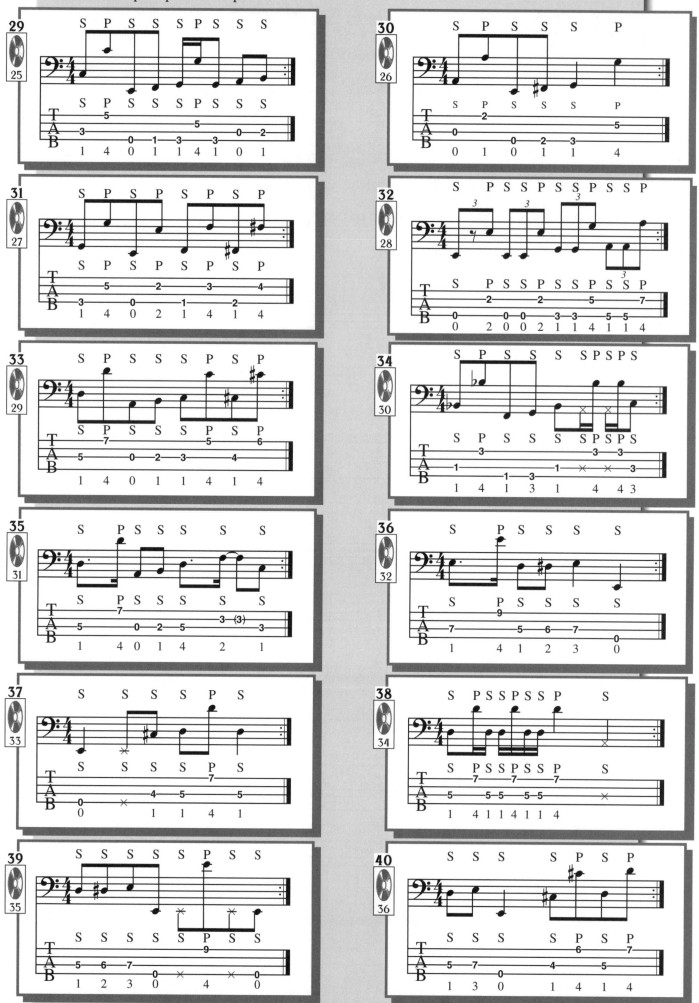

TWO-BAR SLAP & POP LICKS

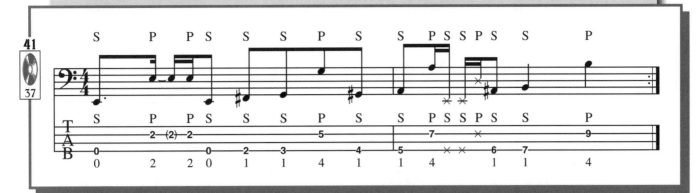

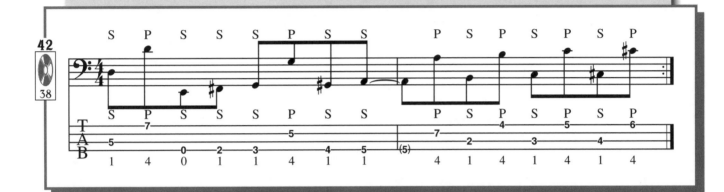

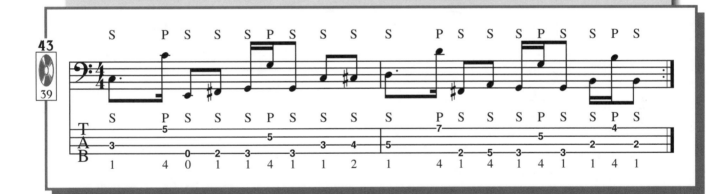

FOUR-BAR SLAP & POP GROOVES

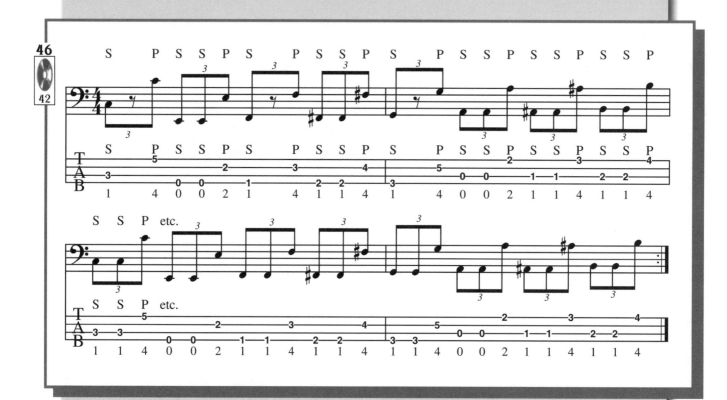

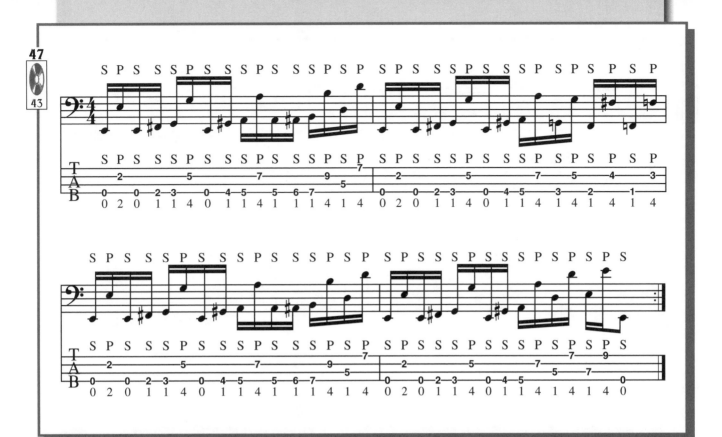

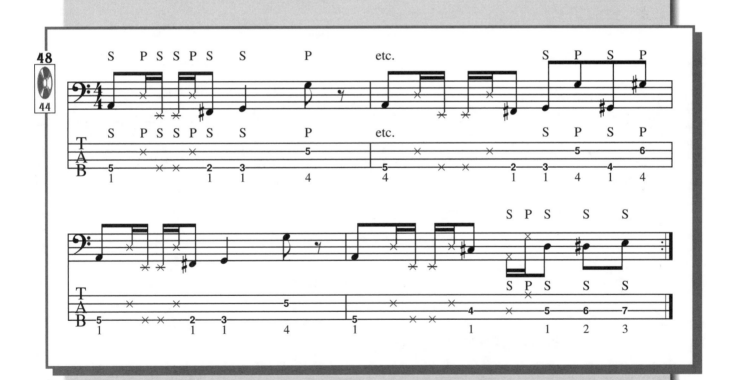

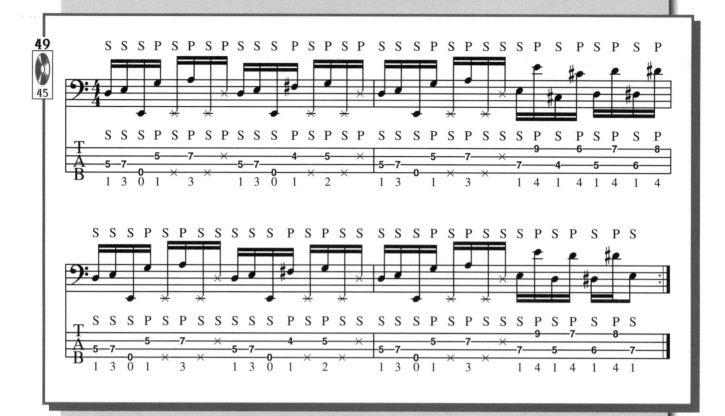

Now, let's add the slide (see page 13) to our slap & pop licks. Make sure to keep the sixteenth notes even throughout.

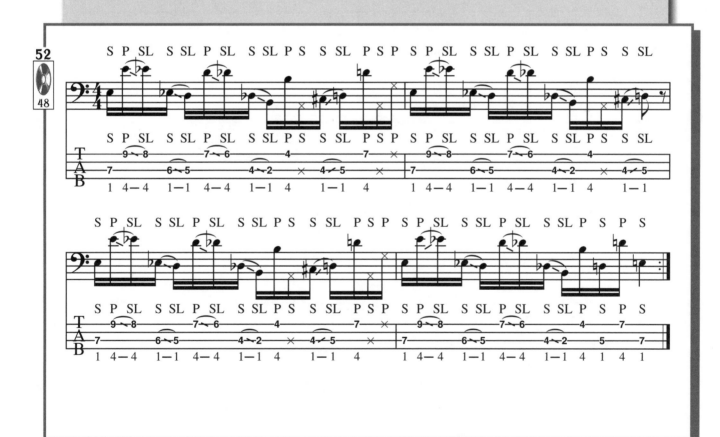

The next few examples may look a lot easier—there are fewer notes and no slides—but watch out for the *syncopated* rhythms (accents shifted to weak or the weak parts of beats)!

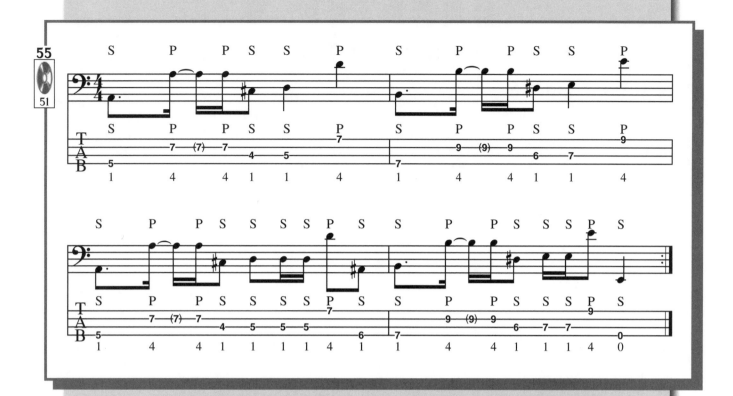

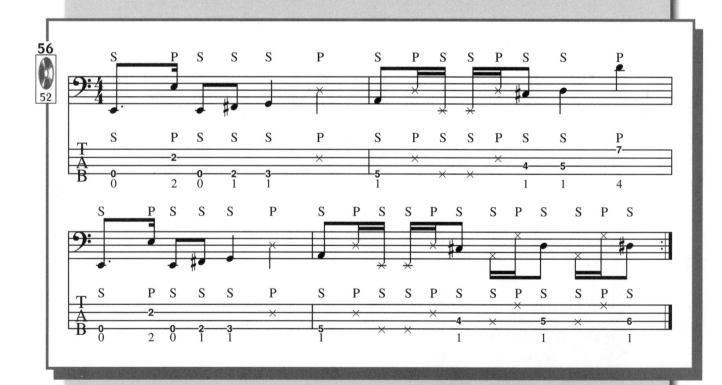

CHAPTER 5
HAMMER-ONS AND PULL-OFFS

HAMMER-ONS

As you learned on page 12, a hammer-on is a legato technique for playing ascending notes with no right-hand articulation. It is indicated with a slur and an "H." In slap & pop technique, a hammer-on usually follows either a slap or a pop, but it is also possible to have two or more hammer-ons in a row, after a single slap or pop. It is a good idea to review page 12 before continuing.

Here are some typical hammer-ons.

PULL-OFFS

As explained on page 12, a pull-off is a legato technique for playing descending notes with no right-hand articulation. It is indicated with a slur and an "S." As with a hammer-on, a pull-off can follow either a slap or a pop, but it can also follow another pull-off or a hammer-on. Again, take a moment to review page 12.

Here are some typical pull-offs.

Photo by Joe Sia • Courtesy of Star File Photo, Inc.

Victor Wooten is a virtuoso bassist who plays with considerable technical ability in a variety of styles. While soloing, he never loses the deep grooves in the music. His work in the 1980s and 1990s with Bela Fleck and the Flecktones, in addition to his dazzling solo recordings, have made him one of today's top bassists.

ONE-BAR LICKS WITH HAMMER-ONS, PULL-OFFS AND SLIDES

Remember that it is best to practice each lick slowly at first. Each example has its own, unique rhythm. Practice with the CD, a metronome or drum machine and lock into the groove, repeating each lick many times.

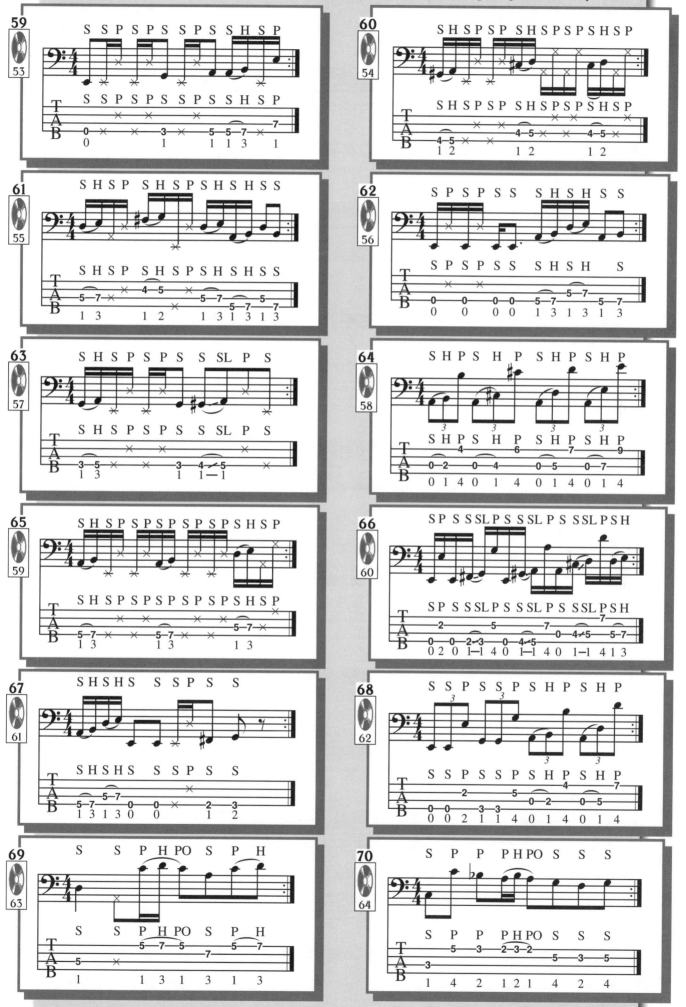

TWO-BAR LICKS WITH HAMMER-ONS, PULL-OFFS AND SLIDES

Practice with a metronome and stay locked into the groove. Play each example slowly at first, and then, when it is mastered, increase the tempo.

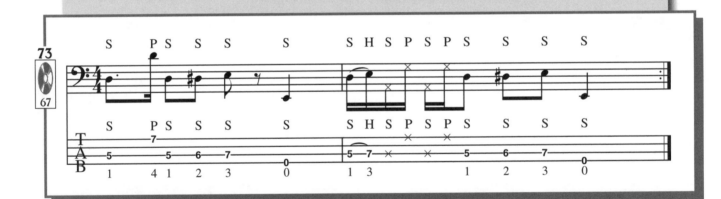

Notice the four-note slur on the first beat of each measure in example 74. A hammer-on is directly followed by a pull-off. Then, the pull-off is followed by a downward slide. The legato techniques combined with the sixteenth-note triplet create an effect of virtuosic embellishment.

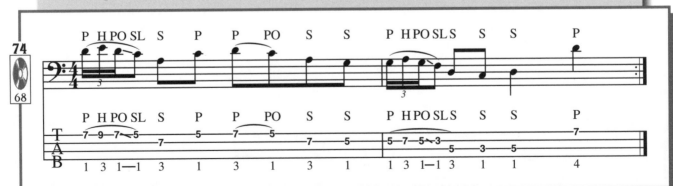

FOUR-BAR GROOVES WITH HAMMER-ONS, PULL-OFFS AND SLIDES

Concentrate on getting a good sound out of each note. Repeat each groove many times and lock into the pulse.

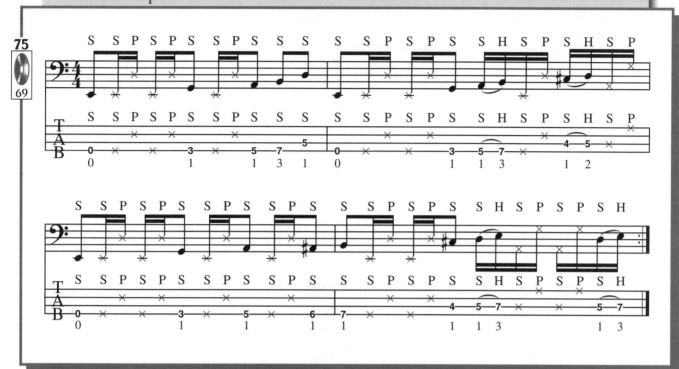

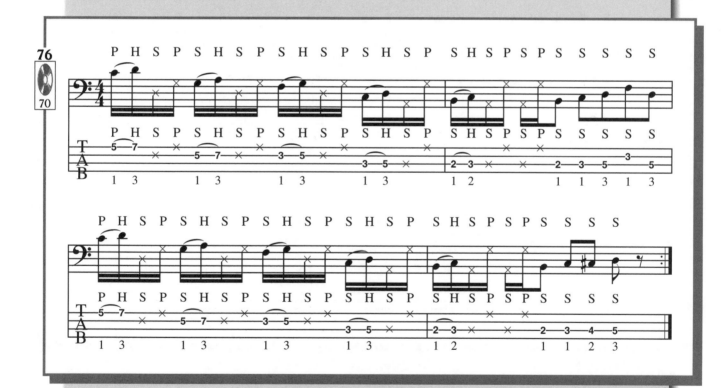

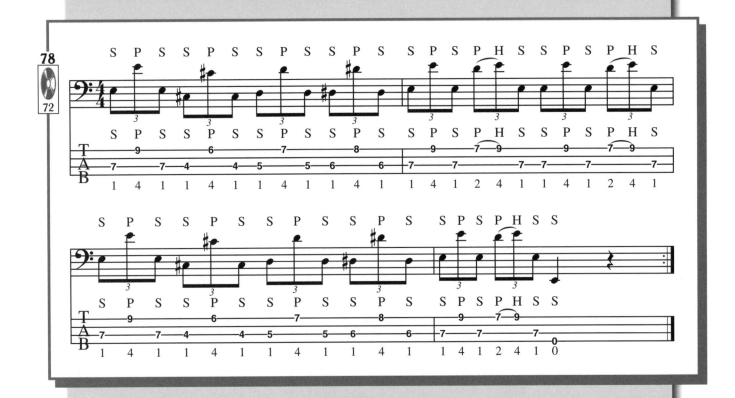

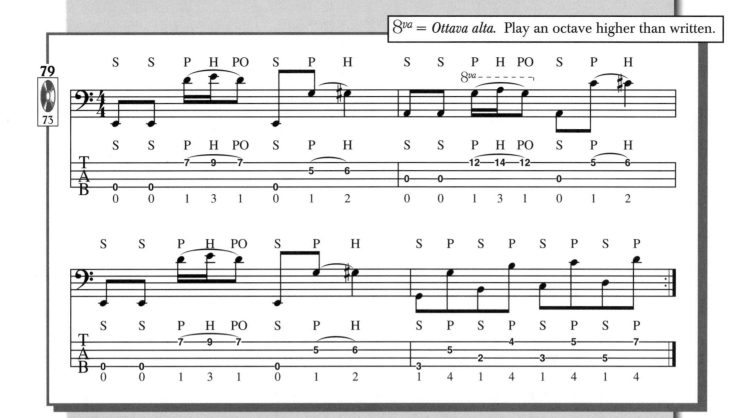

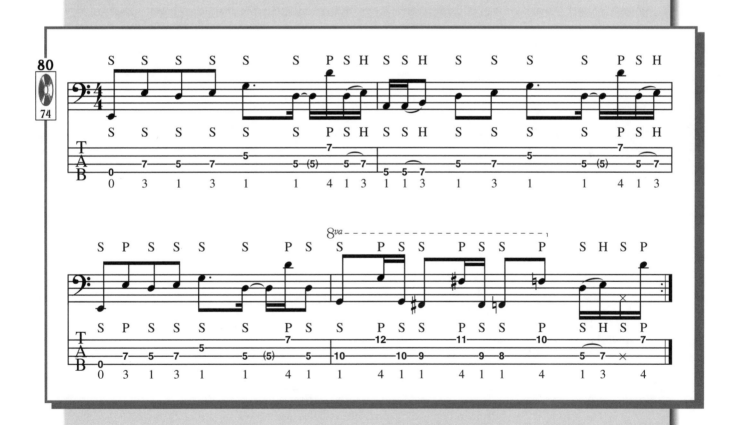

This groove has licks with two hammer-ons in a row. Work on getting a good sound on each hammer-on.

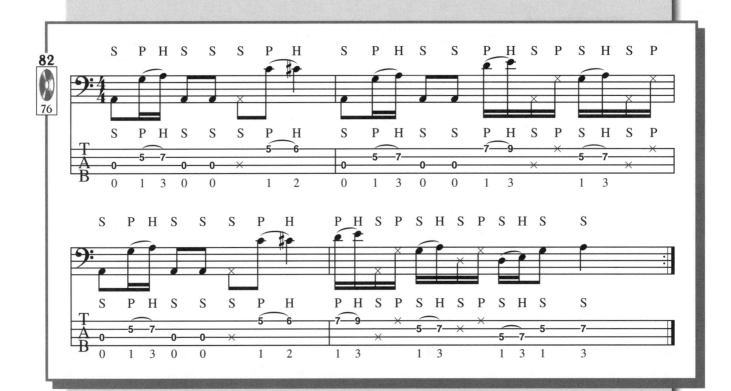

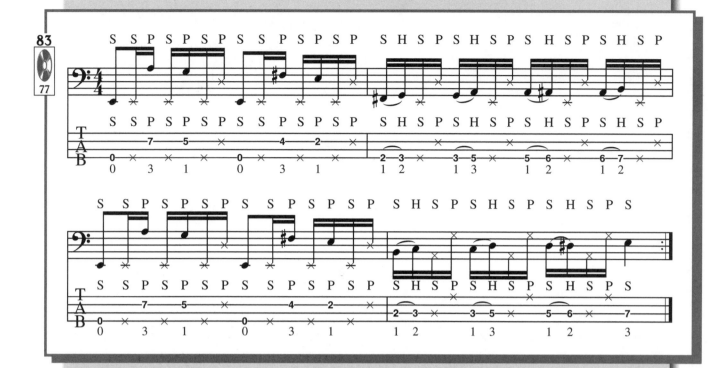

Notice that in example 84, there are slides before some of the notes. Rather than sliding from one specific written note to another, you can add a little "scoop" before a note. While starting slides of this type a whole step below is common, you can choose to slide from further away or closer if you wish.

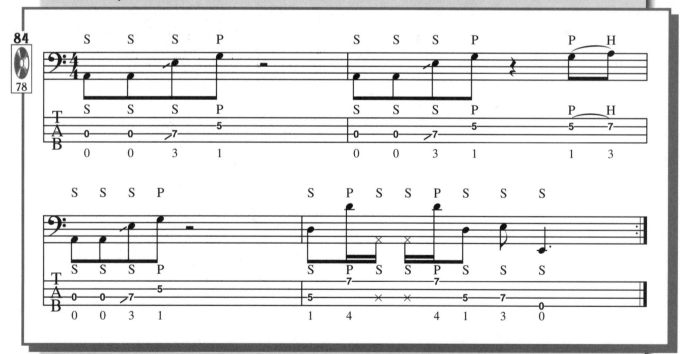

Notice the slide on the fourth beat of the second measure of example 85. It occurs after you play the note. After holding the note for almost its full value, slide your finger down the string. How far you slide is up to you. Experiment. The idea is to give the note an emphasized, end-of-phrase quality.

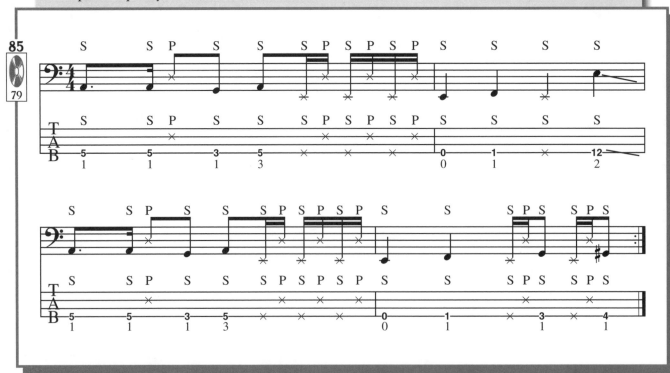

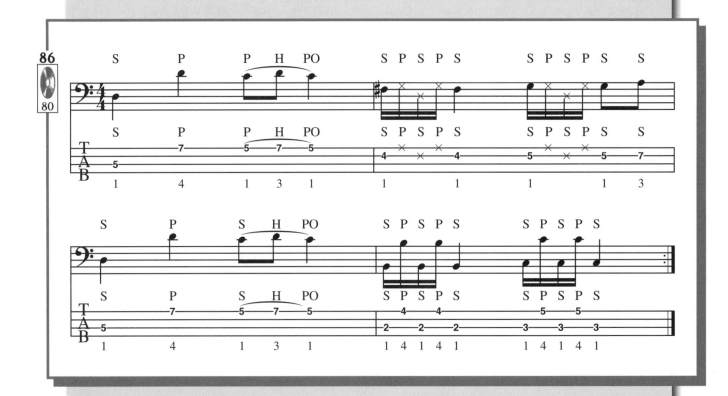

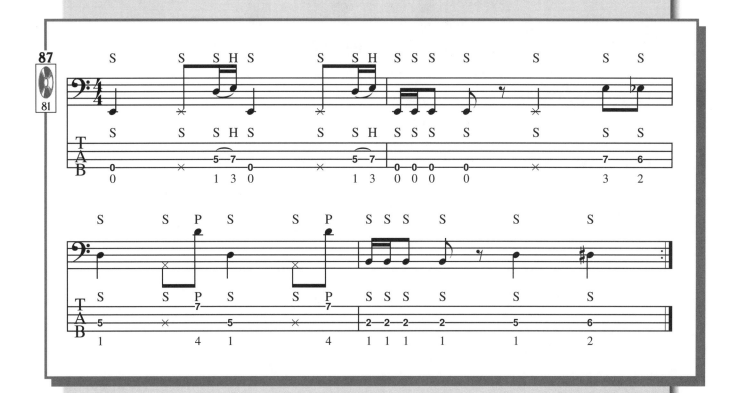

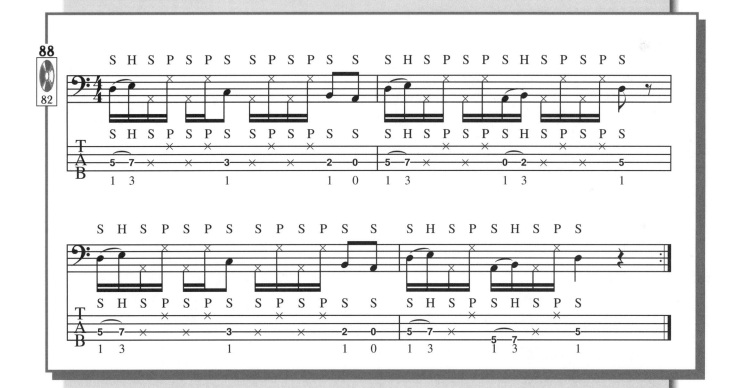

CHAPTER 6
ADVANCED TECHNIQUES

DOUBLE POPS

The slap & pop technique has evolved over the years. Victor Wooten has used the *double pop* technique to create some very cool and interesting bass lines. A double pop is two consecutive popped notes played on two adjacent strings, usually the 2nd and 1st strings.

The double pop is executed by placing the index finger (*i*) of the right hand under the 2nd string and the middle finger (*m*) under the 1st string, pulling both strings, one after the other, away from the fingerboard with enough force that they slap back against the frets.

Here is an example of a double pop.

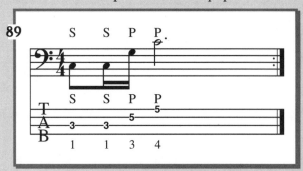

POPPED DOUBLE STOPS

A *double stop* is two notes played simultaneously on a single instrument. From Stanley Clarke's "School Days" to Victor Wooten's "Sinister Minister," there are many great examples of bass lines that include popped double stops.

Here is an example of a popped double stop.

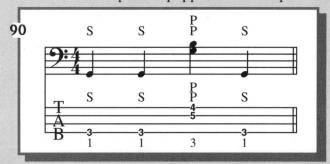

DOUBLE SLIDES

Sliding a double stop can be a great effect, especially after a good, solid popped double stop. The technique is the same as the slide techniques discussed on page 13, except that two left-hand fingers are glided along two strings.

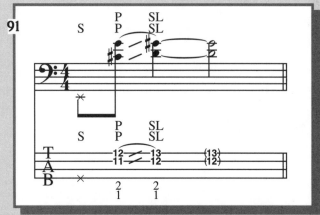

FOUR-BAR GROOVES WITH DOUBLE POPS, POPPED DOUBLE STOPS AND DOUBLE SLIDES

Here are some bass lines that use double pops, popped double stops and double slides. Play each example slowly at first and then pick up the tempo when you are confident. Have fun!

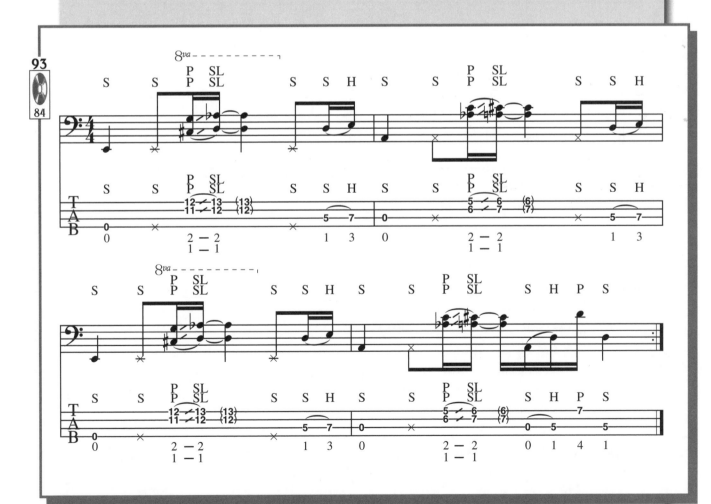

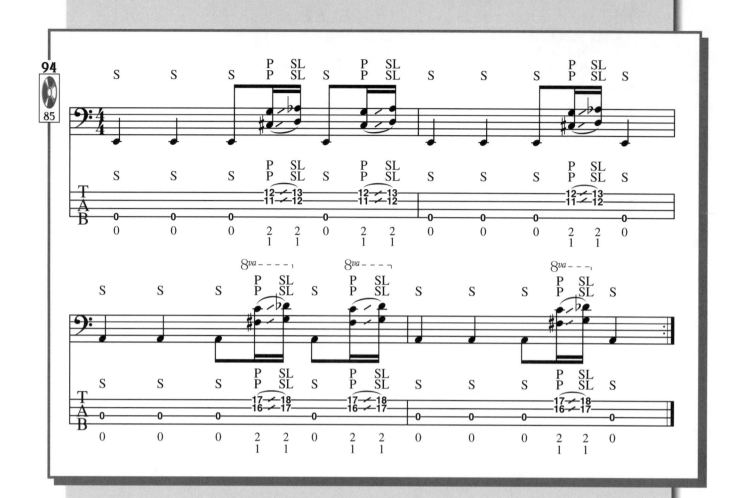

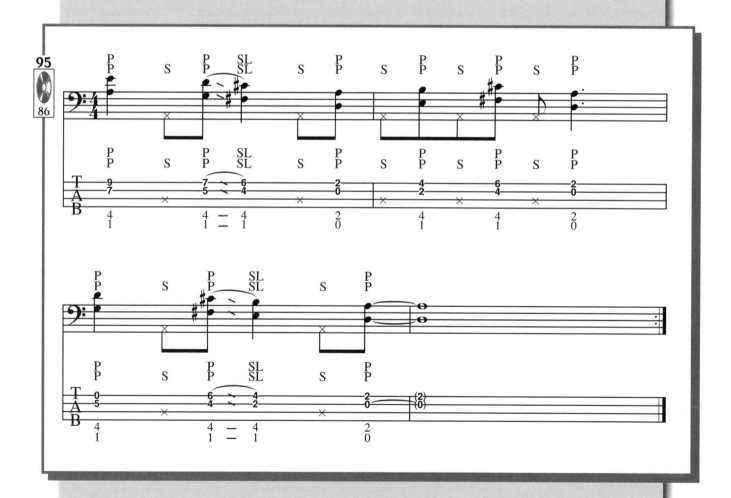

CHAPTER 7
LIBRARY OF FUNK BASS LINES

The following pages contain funk grooves using the techniques covered in this book. Always play slowly at first, then gradually increase the tempo. Have fun playing these lines. Try to incorporate them into your jam sessions and gigs. Keep practicing, and keep playing those funky bass lines.

Flea is the bassist with the Red Hot Chili Peppers. He has also played on other artists' records, such as Young MC's Bust a Move *(1989) and Alanis Morrisette's* You Oughta Know *(1995).*

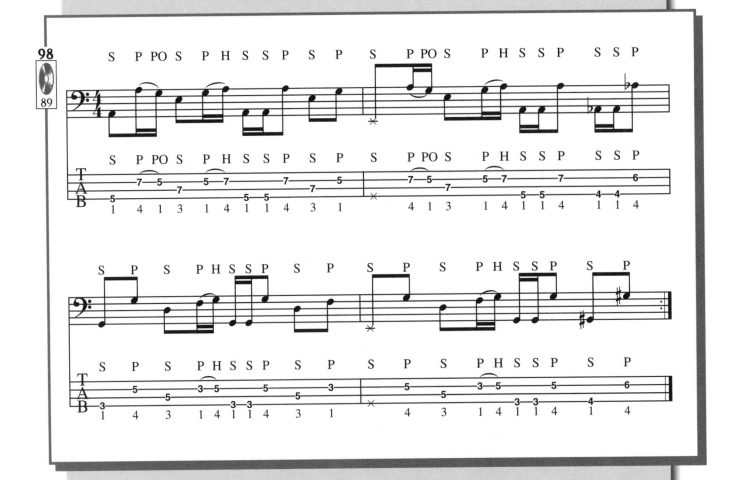

This example includes double pops (see page 38).

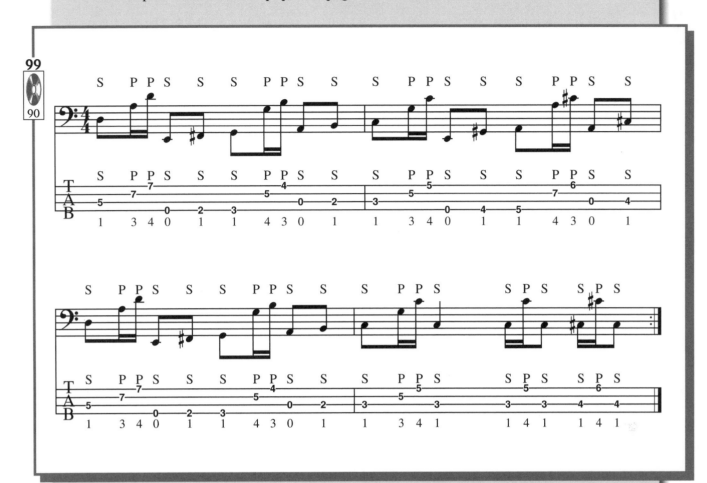

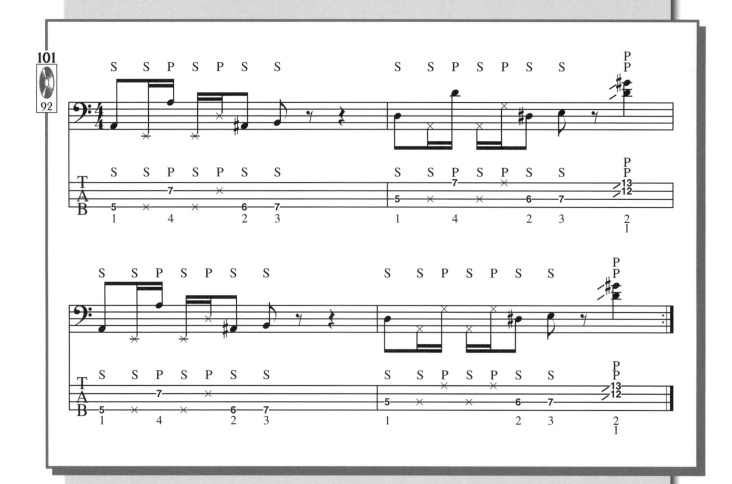

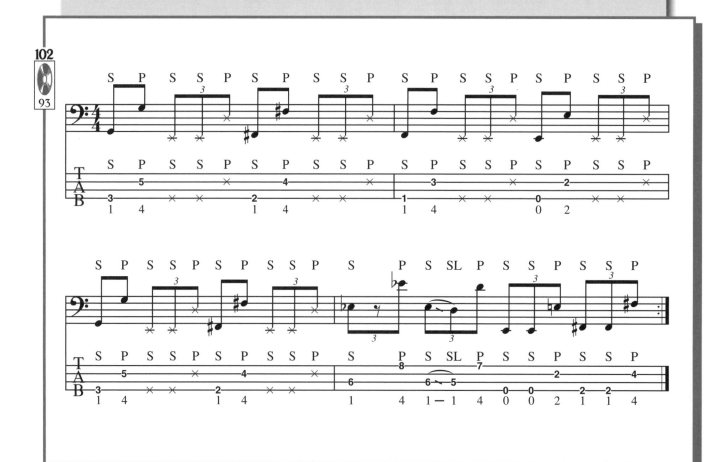

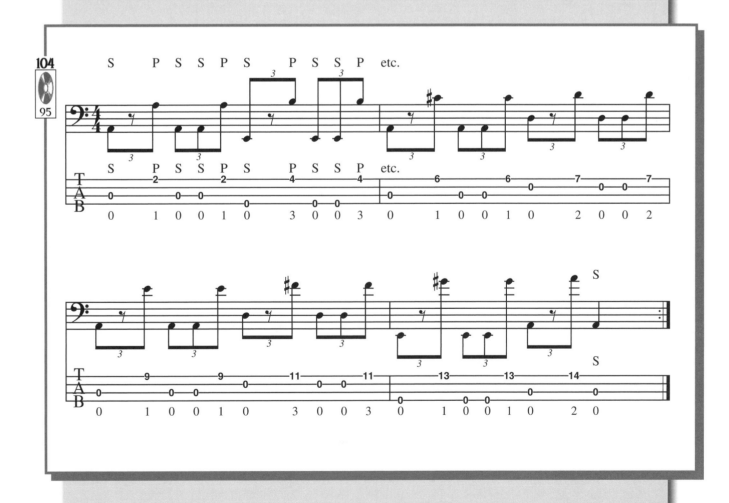

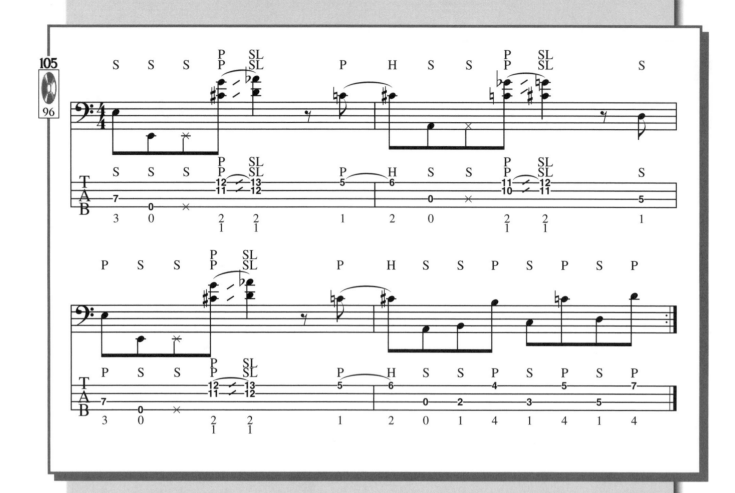

FINAL WORD

Below is a short list of some bass players that you should definitely check out for examples of great slap & pop bass playing. Get your hands on any recordings that include these bass players. These are just a few of the many great bass players that have contributed to the evolution of slap & pop bass playing.

Keep your ears open for others, also!

Bass Player	Band
Stanley Clarke	Return to Forever / solo recordings
Les Claypool	Primus
Bootsy Collins	Parliament / Funkadelics /solo recordings
Flea	Red Hot Chili Peppers
Daryl Jones	Miles Davis
Mark King	Level 42
Michael Manring	solo artist
Marcus Miller	Miles Davis, David Sanborn
Victor Wooten	Bela Fleck / solo recordings

I hope you had a great time learning about the techniques of slap & pop bass playing. Take some of these grooves, put your own twist on them, and come up with some on your own.

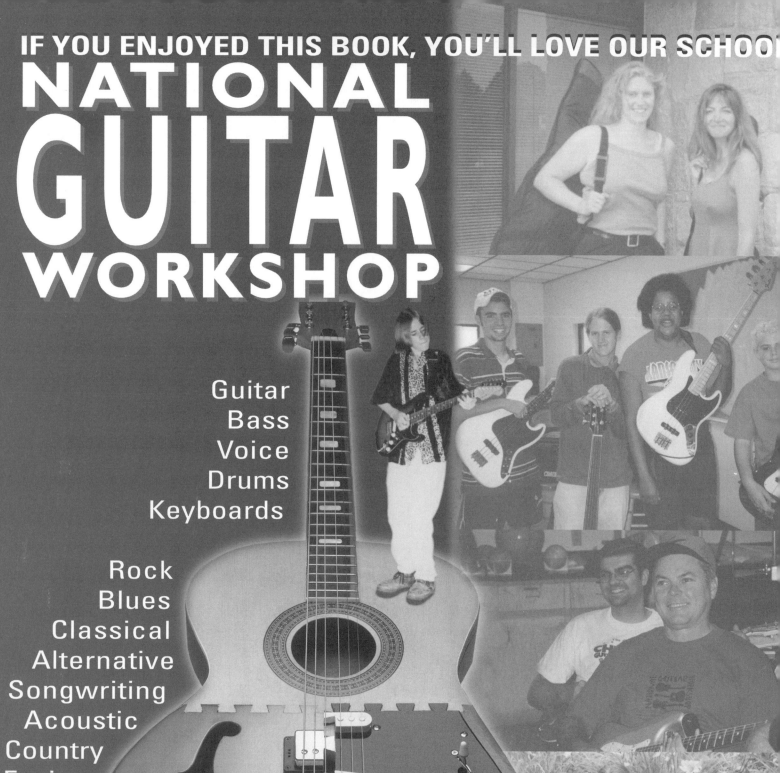